Helping Children to Stay Healthy

From Birth to Three

Ann Roberts and Avril Harpley

 David Fulton Publishers

David Fulton Publishers Ltd
The Chiswick Centre, 414 Chiswick High Road, London W4 5TF

www.fultonpublishers.co.uk
www.onestopeducation.co.uk

First published in Great Britain in 2006 by David Fulton Publishers

10 9 8 7 6 5 4 3 2 1

David Fulton Publishers is a division of Granada Learning Limited.

British Library Cataloguing in Publication Data
A catalogue record for this book is available from the British Library.

ISBN: 1 84312 448 3

EAN: 978 184312 448 1

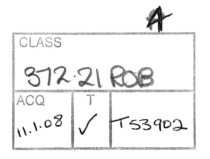
Typeset by FiSH Books, Enfield, Middx.
Printed and bound in Great Britain

Contents

Acknowledgements

Many thanks to the parents of Jasmine Maya, for their kind permission to include her photographs, and all the children and practitioners who have contributed in some way to the making of this book – without them it would not have been possible. Thank you.

Ann and Avril

Introduction

In recent years, health has become an increasingly important issue that features heavily in both political and educational agendas. The purpose of this book is to give practitioners ideas and activities that include and go beyond the simple perception that children's health is solely reliant upon nutrition. It is not just about giving children fresh fruit at snack time or taking them outside when the weather is fine.

Helping children to be healthy means providing support in a comprehensive way – thinking about their physical well-being in a consistent and diagnostic manner, building up good dispositional thinking, supporting and understanding their emotional needs. The well-being of children dominates all they can do, want to do and aspire to do.

Supporting children (when they are in your care) to be healthy is an important responsibility for an early practitioner. Children under three are at their most vulnerable in terms of their physical size and growth and their language capacity. Giving children a healthy start can help prevent problems later on in their lives in terms of their behaviour, well-being, disposition to learn and the growth and development of their body and its functions.

The book refers to the government's *Birth to Three Matters* (DfES, 2002) and uses it as part of its framework. This is to ensure that practitioners do not have to refer to documents other than those with which they are expected to work.

The impact or outcome on children of what we do, say and expose them to should never be underestimated. The adult in control has the responsibility of ensuring the children's human needs are met and it is essential that they get this right. To help with this, we have included staff discussion suggestions and references at the end of each chapter. Finally, references to the National Day Care Standards are made so that practitioners can cross reference their practice to theory and ensure they are meeting and exceeding the standards that they must work to.

Why should we help children to be healthy?

Rising health problems

Childhood obesity (defined as when the total body weight is more than 25% fat in boys and 32% in girls) is on the increase and with this comes associated health problems.

As responsible parents and carers we need to help children realise the benefits of eating healthily and taking exercise.

The importance of a good, balanced diet, with low fat and sugar content cannot be underestimated. Children are reliant on adults to provide their food intake and exercise during the first three years of their life, therefore the role adults play in a child's health is crucial during this time.

Even very young children need daily exercise of their limbs and muscles. A baby has little control of her upper body until she can build up strength in her head, neck and shoulders. Once this is achieved, sitting and moving become easier. When they are on the move toddlers need to walk, march, climb and practise using their lower body.

Effects on well-being

Obesity brings with it problems in children's well-being. Being overweight can result in bullying and cause low self-esteem. Overweight children have a tendency to have high blood pressure, respiratory problems, and cardiovascular conditions. The first cases of adult diabetes have been diagnosed in overweight teenagers.

Good sleep patterns and rest are highlighted as being as important as food in promoting health and well-being. As babies and toddlers grow they need to have a good balance of these to remain healthy.

With children increasingly being moved from their home to childminders or to family members such as their grandparents, or taken to nurseries for their day care, all of these aspects of healthy living are challenged. Consistency is much harder to achieve and standards are not as easily maintained because of the diversity of care, attitudes, values and personal opinions of the adults who are in charge of the children's welfare for a time.

Conclusions

- In their early years, children need the care adults if they are to grow up healthy. Ensuring that the children in your care eat well, sleep well and take exercise will give them the best possible start in life.
- Play is an excellent way to promote exercise. Presenting children with some time in their day in which they have to move and be curious is good for their body and mind.
- Using simple, safe equipment that is age and stage appropriate (balls, hoops, bikes) at an early age engenders a disposition towards exercise as part of the children's lifestyle.
- It is important to recognise that the outside environment is not just a place where children can grow and learn physically, but that their well-being can be developed there too. Frequent outdoor opportunities are needed to develop a healthy child.

- Allowing time for rest is as important as food. Fostering good sleep patterns means that children's energy and concentration levels will be higher, creating greater potential for learning.
- Sufficient consumption of liquids in a day is important as these impact on both body and brain functions.

How to use this book

This book has been written with a practical focus in mind. Practitioners need ideas to use with babies and toddlers. They are busy people and have limited resources at their disposal. The connections made with *Birth to Three Matters* at the beginning of each chapter are designed to support them as they plan and use the documents on a daily basis.

After an introduction, each chapter contains six numbered parts, each one subdivided into sections. The first two sections of each part look at babies and toddlers. The baby section covers from 0 to 18 months and the toddlers' section runs from 18 to 36 months. Both provide practical activities. Obviously the practitioner will recognise that every child is unique and so adaptations to some of the suggested activities will be necessary. Safety is very important and so cautionary advice is offered throughout the book. If children have specialist needs, readers will need to take these into consideration before using the activities and make an informed safety decision on how to use them in their situation.

Following the activities is a section on the outcomes for the child. The points are designed to help us fully recognise the importance of the child in everything that is offered. If we are intending to help children to stay healthy we need to assess how well we are doing this from the child's point of view. Ofsted also focuses on this within its inspection framework and so this will assist practitioners in their evaluations and their preparation for an Ofsted visit.

The focus points that follow are to make us as adults draw some thoughts and feelings together about the practical activities, their purpose, the impact they have and how this can all be built on for the child. They are intended to encourage the reader to consider, question and reflect.

Staff discussion is important. Talking about what we do and trying to make sense of it with others helps us to improve the quality and standard of our work. If we want children to be healthy, we need to see how our role is fitting into the overall picture and how effective we are being.

Finally, each chapter concludes with a list of references and resources. The references are linked to three key documents: *National Standards for Under 8s Day Care and Childminding (Full Day Care)* (DfES/DWP, 2003), *Birth to Three Matters* (2002) and *Every Child Matters* (2003). These are intended to assist the reader in making connections between practice and theory. The resources provide a list of related books, websites and music that practitioners might find useful.

References

DfES (Department for Education and Skills) (2002) *Birth to Three Matters: A Framework to Support Children in their Earliest Years.* London: DfES.

DfES (Department for Education and Skills) (2003) *Every Child Matters.* London: DfES.

Ofsted (Office for Standards in Education)/DfES (Department for Education and Skills) (2003) *Full Day Care: Guidance to the National Standards.* London: DfES.

Emotional well-being

Introduction

The recent government documents *Birth to Three Matters* and *Every Child Matters* encourage the promotion of well-being, one of a child's primary needs. The government of New Zealand introduced this as an essential ingredient of their Early Years National Curriculum, Te Whariki, in the 1990s.

If we, as practitioners, wish to develop well-being, then we have to create the right environment, provide the right experiences and become positive role models. This will help the child to feel secure, develop a strong sense of identity and experience the feeling of belonging. In addition he will become confident, independent and be responsible for making his own decisions. A child needs to be appreciated as an individual, for his uniqueness, to feel that he is quite special and not like anyone else.

This is strengthened by his understanding of his identity as a member of a family, the setting, his language, race and gender. Self-esteem and self-image are central to equal opportunities and how a child relates to others. There is a strong link between well-being and self-esteem. Self-esteem cannot be taught, it is acquired through our experiences connecting the emotions and the mind. It tells a child how he feels about himself and how he believes others see him.

Self-esteem is fragile and can be easily damaged. Even high self-esteem needs to be reinforced. When a child is confident about himself and has his feet planted firmly on the ground, he is better equipped to cope with the knocks and disappointments of life and his performance and potential are enhanced.

> Self-esteem is the key to your life . . . Poor self-esteem is the root cause of all social and personal problems.
> (Murray White, International Council for Self-Esteem: www.esteem-workshops.co.uk)

1. Emotional stability and resilience

Young babies are social beings. They crave close attachments with a special person within their setting

(*Birth to Three Matters*)

Babies

A baby gradually develops a sense of self, the understanding that she is a separate being. Eventually she learns to make choices and do things for herself. In order for this to happen successfully she has to feel secure and trust the people around her. She needs to know who to turn to when distressed or anxious, who will give her comfort and reassurance. The relationships made in these early years will influence the expectations and outcome of future relationships.

Practical activities

Finding time to give a baby your undivided attention helps with bonding and her feelings of security. Introduce a poem or a song and maintain eye contact or touch. Watch for signs that she wishes to end the attention, such as turning away.

● Develop an area of calm with soft colours and quiet music. Have a basket with a variety of soft textures, such as feathers, a fine make-up brush, natural sponge or velvet. Select one and gently rub across her skin. Watch for her responses. As she gets older she may select one herself for you to use.

- Sit two babies on a mat and share the contents of a treasure basket. Note how they communicate and interact with each other.
- Provide a visual stimulus such as a photo of family or carers and watch for signs of recognition.
- Sit two babies opposite each other, talk to them and observe how they reach out or struggle to crawl towards each other.
- Provide a box with interesting items and/or cuddly toys to distract and comfort a distressed child.

Toddlers

During the toddler years the child is trying out his assertiveness and independence by attempting to do things his own way or even saying 'No!' This helps to develop self-confidence, the belief that 'you can do it'. It may mean trying several times before he gets it right and he will need support and encouragement from a significant adult. A toddler may actively seek out another to play with, maybe instinctively recognising they share the same schema.

Practical activities

- Encourage caring attitudes as the children play with dolls or toy animals. Demonstrate how to hold gently, suggest that the doll is tired or hungry. Ensure there are appropriate resources such as blankets and pillows to support the play.
- Introduce the game, 'Blind Man's Bluff', to a small group. This game requires a leap of trust and for some children it could be a distressing activity – having their eyes covered with a scarf may make them feel insecure. Prepare beforehand by playing a simpler game and let the children cover their eyes with their hands.
- Encourage real collaborative play by asking a small group to solve a problem together. For example: a lot of birds visit the outside area and need food and water. How can we look after them? Listen carefully to their suggestions and support with resources and sensitive intervention.

Outcomes for the child

- The emergence of independence.
- Awareness of others.
- Development of friendships.

Focus points

From infancy to three years children make huge steps in relationships as they learn to deal with their emotions, both good and bad. They develop the ability to manage their feelings and as they get older they widen their circle and begin to form close relationships with other children. Experiencing a consistent relationship with a carer helps a young child to handle his feelings.

If a child experiences a number of inconsistent relationships with adults, it may affect his ability to trust and form friendships in later life. Some babies may show signs of distress if held by an unfamiliar carer and some will only respond to one favourite carer. It is important that adults do not take it personally if a baby does not want to come to them.

It is unfortunate that the current fear of child protection issues has made carers hesitant about touching or giving cuddles since close contact, a reassuring touch and warm cuddles are essential for the growth and emotional development of young children.

Staff discussion

Observe your own interactions with children.

- Do you listen attentively, share your interests with them, give genuine praise; do you talk about them over their heads?
- What strategies do you need to support and foster an emerging independence?
- Are the key values in the setting the same for adults and children? Do you feel valued, supported and respected?
- What can you do to build strong and safe relationships with all of the children in your care?

2. Positive relationships

Warm, mutual, affirmative relationships give babies the courage to express their feelings

(*Birth to Three Matters*)

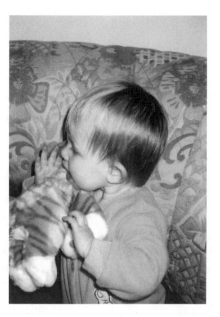

Babies

From the earliest days, babies seek approval from parents and carers. How an adult reacts to them and their behaviour can affect how they deal with situations in later life. Warm and positive reactions promote a confidence in self and pleasure in repeating their actions. A crying baby can sense if her carer is tense, impatient or annoyed and in turn she becomes more stressed and harder to calm.

Practical activities

- Very small babies will need to feel secure and close. A baby carrier will allow the adult to move about the environment while holding the baby safely. She will enjoy the movement and the physical warmth.

- Provide a variety of press and response toys that allow the baby to discover she can make things happen and has power and control over her play.

- If a baby is distressed, give a calm and reassuring massage. Make very small gentle circles around temples, then use thumbs either side of the nose and down to the mouth.

Caution: Do not use oil that is petroleum based.

- During the first year, babies learn that by smiling and laughing they can keep an adult's attention. Increase the smiles with a pleasurable experience such as blowing bubbles.

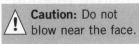

Caution: Do not blow near the face.

Toddlers

Toddlers are not small adults. They are unpredictable — one moment feeling exuberant and independent; the next tearful, insecure and anxious. They are confused about their feelings. They want to reach out and be sociable but cannot always cope with conflict and lack self-control. They do not have the verbal skills to confidently and effectively express their feelings. At times there will be conflict as strong emotions erupt. It is important that the carer does not ignore these feelings as they are very real to the child.

Practical activities

- Plan 'come together' times to reinforce the feeling of belonging and being part of the group. This is essential for a child to develop his sense of well-being and identity.
- Create a home-style environment with soft floor cushions and even sofas where a toddler can choose to chill out and relax quietly on his own.
- Provide large cardboard boxes where children can climb in and disappear and then reappear, experiencing for themselves being temporarily absent and returning.
- Be prepared for tantrums and frustrations. Deal with these seriously, finding out what is upsetting the child and offering an alternative focus: 'Instead of biting, why you don't play with this toy until you feel better?' or 'You decide how long you want to be sad'.
- Take a series of photographs of children during free play. Later show the photographs and ask the children to say what they were doing and how they were feeling.
- Make up stories to reflect their own play experiences, showing ways to behave and react, then talk about their feelings.

Outcomes for the child

- Understanding that it is OK to have a range of emotions.
- Awareness that others have emotions too.

Focus points

We are role models to the children. They see how we treat each other and decode subtle messages through our behaviour and our interactions. We may say one thing yet blatantly do the opposite. Find every opportunity to give genuine praise, recognise the positive and reinforce good behaviour – catch them being good and communicate these events to parents. Children need stability and consistency. It is important for them to know that the way they are treated does not depend on the mood of the adult. If they have known boundaries, it helps to remove anxiety about what is going to happen.

Staff discussion

- How do you communicate persistent problems to parents?
- How do staff manage a child who is distressed?
- Do staff treat each other with respect, thank each other and celebrate their achievements together?

3. Being special to someone

Young babies are social beings. They crave close attachments with a special person in their setting

(*Birth to Three Matters*)

Babies

In an ideal world babies have stable and consistent relationships. They experience close physical contact and feel loved. This lays the foundation for trusting others in the future. During the early years, children discover who they are and how others respond to them.

Practical activities

- It is important to all concerned that the morning hand over is done sensitively and takes place in a calm environment, away from the hustle and bustle in the setting. A positive greeting and a few personal words to the parents can help them at this stressful time.

- Parents should know the name and face of the person who will be looking after their baby; this is someone their baby can form a special attachment with as they develop a consistent and secure relationship. Display photos of key staff in the entrance together with a brief description of them and their duties. Manage staff holidays or absences so that parents are prepared for their baby to be cared for by another.

- Make sure babies' familiar objects are visible as they lie in their cot. Ask the parents for the key words the family use for toileting, sleeping, feeding and use these same phrases during the day.

- Position babies where they have a wide field of vision and face other children so that they feel part of the group. Fix mirrors at their eye level so they can look at themselves and others. After sleep time ensure that a familiar adult is on hand to greet them when they wake.

- Have quiet times during the day: hold the baby safely facing you, look into her eyes and whisper her name, smile and coo. Try a range of facial expressions but watch for signals that say she has had enough.

Toddlers

This is an important stage when toddlers develop their identity and establish their role within the group. Consistent use of their name is a very special part of this process.

Practical activities

- Support each child in making a picture scrap book showing family members, pets and favourite things, captioned with relevant names, relationships and positive statements. Talk about the pictures with each child. There may be a variety of relationships that make up a family.

- Label pegs, drawers, work produced and possessions clearly with their name, in their original alphabet if not English. Attach photographs where appropriate.

- Play the 'Train game': An 'engine driver' picks up passengers who then hold on to a long rope to become the train. The driver walks around and stops to ask each child in turn 'What is your name?', inviting them to join the train by saying 'OK (Ryan) you can join the train.' Limit the number in the group so that the train and the activity are not overlong.

- Sit the children in a circle. Say 'I am (Debbie) and I am sending this ball to (Tony)' and roll the ball. When he (Tony) gets the ball he continues the game and chooses who to roll the ball to, saying their name. With younger toddlers sit in a small tight circle so the ball does not 'run away'.

- Keep interesting items of clothing in a special box for dressing up; include clothing from a variety of cultures. Allow the children to wear the clothes all day if they wish as they try out characters.

Outcomes for the child

- While working and playing with others, children are developing social skills.
- The use of a child's name helps to develop a strong sense of identity.
- Dressing up and playing a role develops creativity and imagination.

Focus points

In our multicultural society we need to value race and culture. Ensure that adults learn and use key words in the children's home language such as hello, toilet, drink, tired/sleepy and goodbye. If you find pronunciation difficult, write out how it sounds to you in English. This is especially important with a child's name. Group same language speakers together at set times. Encourage them to bring objects from home to talk about at special times and incorporate these into daily activities.

Staff discussion

- Be aware that some children may not take to you or you to them. How would you handle this?

- How can you manage staff absences and holidays so that parents and children are prepared for them to be cared for by another staff member?

4. Being able to express feelings

Provide stories, pictures and puppets, which allow children to experience and talk about feelings

(Birth to Three Matters)

Babies

Before children develop speech they are sensitive to an adults' emotions through the sound of their voice, gestures and facial expressions. Faces are very important to babies – eyes in particular – as these transmit feelings. In turn they have learnt to communicate signs to express how they are feeling and their needs. Children's responses are individual and unique.

Practical activities

- Observe the sounds and facial expressions a baby makes when cuddled, changed or fed. Notice how the baby responds to separation, anger or frustration. Does she protest and cry or become quiet and withdrawn? Perhaps she even appears to be 'not bothered' and detached?

- Ensure there are familiar objects to distract and interest the baby. To accustom a baby to separation and reunion play the game 'Peek-a-boo', where you hide your face and then make it reappear. This game can be extended by using a simple puppet and a curtain.

- With a colleague play 'Rock-a-bye baby', as described in Chapter 2.

- Alternatively play 'Drop and pick-up' where the baby is in charge of dropping an object and you return it, over and over again.

- Collect three or four photos of the baby and family members. Glue these onto a piece of strong card. Slip into a plastic folder and punch holes in the top, attaching the sheets together with a ribbon. Turn the photos over and point to her photos. Observe her responses, which ones she enjoys or wants to look at again.

Toddlers

Toddlers will be experiencing a whole range of new situations and emotions but may not have the language skills to express how they feel. Be aware that this frustration can provoke verbal and physical outbursts.

Practical activities

- Use stories to introduce the vocabulary that describes feelings such as *Angry Arthur*, *Timid Tim and the Cuggy Thief*, or *My Many Coloured Days* (see 'Resources').

- Develop role play and discussion. Collect photographs of people showing a range of expressions and discuss them with the children. Ask them to look in a mirror and copy a face. Ask, 'If the face looks like this how do you think the person is feeling? How can you tell? Why do you think he is feeling like this? Have you ever felt this way? What did you feel like when . . . ?

- Provide activities that help children to work through or control their anger and frustration such as being able to pound dough or bang a drum.

- Introduce a coloured block as a symbol. For example, an orange block says 'I feel OK'. Gradually introduce other blocks to show sadness, anger, excitement, etc. Let one of the children choose the block that describes his feelings today and say why he has chosen it. End sessions by passing around a smile. Make eye contact with a child, smile and say 'Pass it on'. He grabs the smile and passes it on. Keep the group small so that everyone has a chance to participate.

- Introduce a wide range of music and encourage the children to express themselves (see 'Resources').

Outcomes for the child

- Social skills improve as children become aware of others' feelings.
- Children learn to co-operate and become part of a group.
- They begin to explore their own identity and self-awareness.

Focus points

Be aware that parents may be experiencing a whole range of emotions when leaving their baby for the first time. They may even feel jealous of their baby's attachment to the key carer. At reunion times make sure the baby is relaxed and happy to see them. Before the baby is left in full-time care it is beneficial to introduce the carer and the new environment gradually. For example, the parent should leave her briefly and return, building up to ten minutes and then longer. Try to alleviate this sensitive time by making sure the separation is in a calm environment and not rushed, the baby is handed over to a familiar carer and the parent can be reassured by phoning or returning to check if he is concerned.

Staff discussion

- Review your resources and identify stories that will help children to recognise their own emotions, fears or happiness and will promote discussion.
- Current research suggests that music, Mozart in particular, has beneficial effects on young children's intellectual development by strengthening mental pathways and developing cognitive skills.
- Collect a variety of music that provides an outlet for physical expression and emotions. Use quieter, reflective music to calm and soothe children after strenuous activity. Discover music that tells a story, such as 'Peter and the Wolf', to concentrate their listening skills and develop their imagination (see 'Resources').
- Be aware that some music may excite the children and encourage vigorous physical movements. How can you channel this expression into a positive response?

5. Developing a healthy dependency

When young children have a close relationship with a caring and responsive adult, they explore from a safe place to which they can return
(Birth to Three Matters)

 Babies

Babies are vulnerable and totally dependent on adults to meet their needs. They need to feel secure and safe, knowing they can trust their key carer.

Practical activities

- Develop a calm environment. Babies are acutely aware of subtle signals of body language, voice and gestures and can feel tension or stress in an adult.

- Organise a regular pattern to the day so that the babies know what to expect and when. During transition times have each baby's favourite toy close by, pretend to change teddy's nappy or wash his face. Babies may get very stressed if their needs are not met quickly. Ideally arrange for them to be cared for by the same key person.

- Once the baby starts to crawl build trust with a gentle game of chase, crawling after her and giving a cuddle or a tickle when you catch her.

- Hold baby firmly and gently swing while singing 'Rock-a-bye baby'.

- Gradually introduce new items into her environment such as colourful shapes, mobiles and music.

- Babies need time to explore, discover and practise. This can mean doing the same thing over and over, for example continually throwing objects out of the cot to be picked up, or expressing the desire for an activity to be repeated by asking 'Again?'

Toddlers

A toddler is aware that he is separate from other people but may still need to hold on tight to his significant carers. He may develop strong attachments to certain items and be upset if he has to part with them. Carers need to be guided by each child's rhythms for food, sleep and activity.

Practical activities

- Young children learn through imitation or copying. Use role play, puppets and stories to help children develop social skills and learn acceptable behaviour.

- Toddlers may be anxious about strangers so introduce new people and new situations gradually, giving them time to get used to them.

- Encourage the children to gain confidence with physical skills by using low level apparatus for balance, soft ball play and climbing skills or the thrill of a swing.

- Create a simple picture diary of daily routine events, for example washing hands, toileting, eating and playing. Remind the toddler of what happened and share the events with him. Develop this into an 'I can' or an 'I helped' book. Collect pictures and photographs of ordinary daily events and display.

- Make a display to celebrate the toddler's achievements, for example hanging coloured leaves on a branch as each new skill is learnt.

- Extend hiding and searching games so that the toddler has to look further afield.

Outcomes for the child

- Development of confidence and self-esteem.
- Increased awareness of others and their needs.
- Socialisation – beginning to play alongside each other or in small groups.

Focus points

Remember that the most vital resource in the setting are the adults. Maintaining positive links with a child's family is essential. Even though the baby or the toddler appears to be developing independence and spends more and more time away from her carer there will be times when she suddenly becomes anxious and needs to be reassured you are still there. She will explore from a safe place, knowing she can return to you. Some children will still need their special comforter or toy. Hearing a favourite song or playing a favourite game over and over is both comforting and reassuring. Encourage the learning of new skills with small, achievable steps and genuine praise to give a sense of achievement. Exploring strategies to develop confidence and self-esteem will help a toddler to become more independent.

Listen and watch so that you can respond to her interests and plan the next steps carefully. Try to keep a balance between over-stimulation and over-protection.

Staff discussion

- How are staff rotas organised so that daily routines of toileting, hygiene and eating are undertaken with familiar carers? How are toilet accidents taken care of?
- How do you deal with clashes: when a developing, independent toddler challenges you and refuses point blank to conform how do you react?
- How do staff support children with disabilities?
- Review your stories and tapes and list those that help children to become more independent.

6. Developing a healthy independence

As children learn to do things for themselves they gain confidence, knowing that an adult is close by, ready to support and help if needed.
(Birth to Three Matters)

Developing independence is an exciting time when children become more mobile and begin to display their individual personalities. General development stages are predictable, but each child has its own timetable – a unique pattern of growth and behaviour that needs individual support and guidance.

Babies

A baby's development changes rapidly and dramatically during the first year of her life. From being able to hold up her head she will learn to crawl and even walk. She is no longer a passive receiver but has the freedom to explore the world, become active and to try things out for herself. The practitioner's role is crucial: to plan and organise the provision of safe but interesting materials and objects and then support the baby through responsive interaction.

Practical activities

● Examine heuristic play opportunities, often referred to as 'treasure baskets' (see 'Resources'). Place interesting or familiar objects just out of reach so that the baby has to move towards them. Add a new object or take one away, observing her response.

- Babies are curious about other children. Encourage social interaction by facilitating activities with other babies and other adults such as water play or joining in with finger rhymes.

- Encourage simple social skills such as learning greetings and waving bye-bye.

- Increase self-help skills where children can gain confidence and begin to take control, for example learning how to wash and dry their hands, put on their coat or use the toilet. Give genuine praise when they achieve a task and encourage them to say to you 'I can do it!'

Toddlers

Toddlers are active and curious, often unpredictable; they are impulsive and lack self-control yet have an increasing need to be with other children. The concepts of sharing and fair play may not have developed so there could be conflict struggles for independence.

Practical activities

- When children work together duplicate some resources to ease frustrations.

- Use a novelty egg timer to show how to share fairly: 'When the ringer goes your time is up!' Challenge them by asking 'Who can tidy up before the pinger goes?'

- Play will be the starting point to develop many social skills. Provide child-sized tools, such as a dustpan and brush so they can help to tidy up. They learn best by 'doing'. A doll's tea party is an ideal time to reinforce table manners. Initiate discussions about how we care for each other when bathing dolls and show where to find towels, sponges or carry water carefully.

- Create a treasure hunt game to help toddlers find resources in the room. Label resources clearly with text and pictures, making sure that the children can see these indicators.

- Take advantage of outdoor play where active toddlers can run, play and shout without inhibitions. Here they can develop mastery over materials and objects and manipulative exercises that can be stored for future use. They learn best by doing and having first-hand experiences. Crawling through a tunnel may help a child to overcome fears while exercising whole body muscles.

Outcomes for the child

- Emerging personal, social and emotional skills.
- Awareness of own needs and identity.

Focus points

As you allow them to take the initiative and explore their environment it is essential that you carry out a risk assessment to ensure it is a safe environment. Knowing familiar routines and developing an understanding of basic rules will provide toddlers with security. They find it difficult to express their needs and this can give rise to misunderstandings and even physical outbursts. The practitioner's skill in being alert to signs of restlessness and offering diversions can help to prevent a difficult situation from developing. These misunderstandings can be very important to a child so the adult needs to be able to listen carefully, giving time and attention to each child.

Staff discussion

- What basic rules need to be in place to avoid conflict?
- How can you help a toddler take the initiative and support him to develop self-control and responsibility for his own behaviour?

References

DfES (Department for Education and Skills) (2002) *Birth to Three Matters: A Framework to Support Children in their Earliest Years.* London: DfES.

DfES (Department for Education and Skills) (2003) *Every Child Matters.* London: DfES.

Ofsted (Office for Standards in Education)/DfES (Department for Education and Skills) (2003) *Full Day Care: Guidance to the National Standards.* London: DfES.

Resources

Campbell, D. (2002) *The Mozart Effect: Tapping the Power of Music to Heal the Body, Strengthen the Mind and Unlock the Creative Spirit.* London: Hodder & Stoughton.

Goldschmied, E. and Jackson, S. (2003) 'Heuristic play with objects', in *People under Three: Young Children in Day Care.* London: Routledge.

Goleman, D. (1996) *Emotional Intelligence: Why it Can Matter More than IQ.* London: Bloomsbury.

Oram, H. (1982) *Angry Arthur*. London: Random House.

Prater, J. (1993) *Timid Tim and the Cuggy Thief*. London: Random House.

Seuss, Dr (1998) *My Many Coloured Days*. London: Random House.

Tomlinson, J. (1973) *The Owl Who Was Afraid of the Dark*. London: Puffin Books.

Forest Schools – www.forestschools.com

Esteem workshops – www.esteem-workshops.co.uk

Music

Claude Debussy, 'La Mer' or 'Clair de lune'

Sergei Prokofiev, 'Peter and the Wolf'

Camille Saint-Saëns, 'The Carnival of the Animals'

Mozart

2 Growing and developing

Introduction

Adequate food and drink are essential for the development and well-being of children. In the beginning a baby's needs are met by her mother's milk, or formula. During her first weeks of life a baby will grow at the rate of 200 grams a day, and by six months this has almost doubled. Once a toddler starts to walk and become active, his energy is high and he grows in leaps and bounds.

Children all develop at different rates so adults who care for them should be aware of the development sequence and treat them as individuals. Observe and encourage the correct crawling patterns before walking as missing out the key steps of crawling has implications later on and has been linked to dyslexia.

Water is essential to both babies and toddlers; it should always be available, even for those babies who cannot yet communicate. Babies have sensitive gut linings so should be introduced slowly to new food. As young children's stomachs are small meals should be available 'little and often'.

During the growing period physical activity is essential for the development of strong bones and muscles. They need to be encouraged to develop both gross and fine motor skills. This requires patience and practice. Supportive adults need to explore ways to offer opportunities to encourage control, co-ordination and balance.

Sleep is as important as food. Every child needs safe, comfortable and well-monitored sleep opportunities. Tiredness, hunger and discomfort are barriers to learning.

1. Being well nourished

Young babies thrive when nutritional and emotional needs are met
(*Birth to Three Matters*)

Babies

A healthy diet is needed to nourish the mind as well as the body. Without strong muscles and bones the essential development of grasping and holding skills may be delayed and affect those skills required for writing. Vision and hearing also depend on good nutrition and these are integral to language development. Links have also been made between poor nutrition and behaviour. Initially milk will supply all the nutrients a baby needs.

Practical activities

- Current research suggests that even young babies can be taught to use hand signals to communicate when they are hungry, have finished eating or want some more. Watch for their special signs that communicate when they are hungry or have had enough.

- Weaning is a messy and slow process. Try to introduce new tastes and textures such as crunchy, creamy, crumbly, mashed, pureed and tiny chopped foods. Avoid salty or sugary foods from the start. A mashed banana can be added to make foods sweeter and more palatable.

  Caution: Be very aware that babies can choke easily. Never leave them to eat alone. Do not offer anything larger than a $\frac{1}{4}$-inch cube. Preferably grind or chop food.

- Provide tap water that has been boiled and then cooled.

- Provide parents with information about the food their baby has eaten during the day and how they responded to it.

Toddlers

This is a period of growth with intense activity and rest. A toddler can't eat large amounts of food at any one time, so little and often is the theme. If offering full day care, provide a wide range of food that covers the essential calories and nutrients; protein, vitamins and minerals. This will include cereals, fresh fruit and vegetables, meat, fish and eggs. Continue to encourage them to drink boiled water rather than fruit juices.

Practical activities

- Provide variety by offering the same foods prepared in a different way, for example eggs can be boiled, scrambled, mixed with herbs. Introduce the story of 'Humpty Dumpty'. Did he fall or was he pushed?

- Break a fresh egg and show the children what it looks like inside, then compare it to a hard boiled egg. Decorate hard boiled eggs with Humpty faces. Scramble eggs or make into an omelette.

- Encourage the children to help make egg sandwiches. Cut bread into different shapes with a pastry cutter, slice the eggs, half and quarter them or mash them with mayonnaise; fill pitta bread with egg and cress.

- Create picnic baskets with tiny sandwiches and tiny strips of carrots and courgettes, using a julienne cutter. Lay out a cloth and plates for toys and dolls to have a picnic. Introduce polite table manners and sharing with phrases such as 'Please' and 'Thank you', 'Would you like . . . ?', 'May I have . . . ?

- Use stories linked to food and eating to connect with children's own habits.

> **Caution:** Limit salt and salty products and sugar. Be aware that nuts can cause choking in young children. Check additives and E numbers on processed foods and biscuits.

Outcomes for the child

- Helping to prepare foods encourages hand–eye co-ordination and helps to develop manipulative skills.
- Making choices and showing preferences encourages independence.
- Satisfaction of 'doing it for themselves'.
- Development of manners and social interaction.

Focus point

Feeding and enjoying food is a close bonding time for both children and carers but a number of points need to be observed. If a mother is still breastfeeding, try to facilitate a quiet area where she can do this in private. Provide a cushion to support the baby, a stool to lift the mother's feet, a glass of water to replenish fluids and somewhere she can wash her hands. If using expressed milk, make sure every bottle is labelled clearly with the baby's name and the date and time it was expressed.

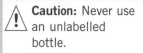 **Caution:** Never use an unlabelled bottle.

- Maintain close supervision whenever babies and young children are eating. They can choke easily and quickly.

- Ensure food is cut up into very small pieces.

- Ensure a qualified First Aider is on site.

- Be aware of food allergies. Settings must have clear records of every child's allergies, and while respecting their privacy, all staff should be aware of children's allergy profiles. Adverse food reactions can be caused for a variety of reasons; therefore records should be checked and updated on a regular basis and counter signed by a senior member of staff. Some settings have a 'nut free' zone indicated by clear visual signs.

- Be extra vigilant over sterilising equipment and the cleanliness of all food containers.

- Encourage children to wash their hands before and after eating

- Be aware of the cultural differences associated with food and religious practices.

Staff discussion

- Are staff aware of the variety of ways sugar is described in packaged foods? The words sucrose, glucose, honey, dextrose, maltose, syrup all indicate sugar content. 'No added sugar' often means they contain aspartame or artificial sweeteners.

- Do staff keep a record of children's cultural background that indicates particular food/religious practices?

- Have staff checked the guidelines available from the Food Standards Agency?

2. Healthy eating habits

Treat mealtimes as an opportunity to help children to enjoy their food and become independent in feeding themselves

(Birth to Three Matters)

Babies

Healthy eating habits are developed during early childhood. A setting has a key role in helping children and their parents discover how to make healthy choices and promote a balanced diet.

Eating with a small group will encourage children to interact with each other, developing their social behaviour.

Practical activities

- Once a baby is weaned watch her mouth movements and hand and body movements to see if she is ready to feed herself. Place small items of food on her tray and encourage her to pick them up. Observe carefully. For example, try her with peas, corn, raisins or small pieces of fruit cut into 1/4-inch cubes.

- Make sugarless jellies in different colours. Use natural food colouring and observe if she shows a preference. Does the colour of the jelly affect her choice? Add tiny pieces of fruit to jellies.

- Provide food cut into different shapes and textures. Introduce strips of vegetables that she can hold and chew upon. As she starts teething provide cubes of frozen fruit puree that she can suck on and cool her gums.

- Explore the many varieties of bread available from around the world, such as nan, pitta bread, brown bread and serve with spreads or dips.

Toddlers

Mealtimes can become a battleground and some children reject meals or a particular food for a variety of emotional reasons. It is very important to work closely with parents and to know how they handle difficult eating situations or if there is a medical condition which affects their child's eating.

Practical activities

- Introduce a family style meal, with one adult and a small group. Make sure that the adult eats the same food as the children and has nothing that they are not allowed such as hot coffee.

- Create an attractive eating area. Encourage the children to set the table and clean up afterwards. Place the food in the centre of the table and allow the children to help themselves. Provide plates and containers that are lightweight and can be easily reached. Ensure the chairs and table are the right height: chairs should allow the feet to reach the floor and table needs to be at about waist- or mid-chest height.

- Initiate conversation, manners and polite behaviour. Introduce simple rules, for example only eat when seated at the table, sharing food fairly.

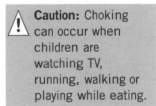

Caution: Choking can occur when children are watching TV, running, walking or playing while eating.

- Introduce a new fruit or vegetable every week; look for those from other countries as well as local produce. Touch it, smell it, taste it, describe it and draw a picture of it, make a model of it.

- Look for a story, song, poem or picture about food and use as a starting point. For example, 'I will never, not ever, eat a tomato' (see 'Resources'). Buy a selection of different varieties of tomatoes – different sizes, shapes and colours. Discuss them together: do they all taste the same?

- Allow the children to discover the many ways a tomato can be eaten. Slice it thinly, chop it finely, mash into soups and sauces, add herbs, or juice it.

Outcomes for the child

- Beginning to be aware of the diversity of foods and variety of tastes and textures.
- Developing an increasing ability to make choices and show preferences.
- Developing independence and self-control.
- Developing positive social interaction and turn taking.

Focus points

To prevent future dietary problems avoid using food as a reward. Find alternatives such as verbal praise, stickers, a special activity or applause. Investigate how to plan menus using the major food groups needed to meet the daily requirements of the key nutrients for toddlers two years and over. Use large paper plates and divide these into sections to show food groups:

- Up to 6 servings of grains/bread, 3 small portions of vegetables, 2 small portions of fruit, 2 small portions of milk and proteins.
- A limited amount of fats, sweets and salt.
- Look to include foods that contain Vitamins A and C, minerals, iron-rich foods and calcium.

Over one week colour the areas on the plates to show the food groups eaten each day. Liaise with parents and encourage them to share information about their diet and culture.

Staff discussion

- Review how you offer snacks and food in your setting. Are the children able to eat when they are hungry or only at a specific time? Do you try to make snack time fun and exciting by having picnics or a finger buffet?
- Investigate the many ways you can serve a carrot: mashed into a mound, chopped, cubed, cut into circles, sliced very thinly, shredded, juiced, raw or cooked.
- Do you shop for healthy options and locally produced products?

3. Sleep as nourishment

For babies and children, rest and sleep is as important as food
(*Birth to Three Matters*)

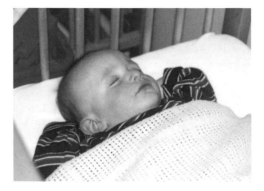

Babies

An average baby sleeps 13.9 hours at six months old. This decreases in toddler-hood to about 12 hours. This reduction in sleep time is not spread out equally during the day and night; therefore babies and toddlers will require sleep facilities in childcare during the day. The space children sleep in is important to them and to their parents. Parents need to be assured that their child is safe. In day care, staffing may change as the child sleeps – staff go on breaks, finish shifts. Good sleep patterns and rest times are important.

Practical activities

- At the foot or top of each cot put a square of double-sided Velcro. This is to attach a photo and short summary about each child. This is very useful when staff show parents around, when staff patterns alter in the day, or in the event of a fire. The cards are stored in a wallet or box and as each child is laid down to sleep the member of staff puts up the occupant of that cot's information. This helps everyone know a child's needs especially at sleep time. For example, Sam likes his comforter (small blanket sample) and he likes to have his back rubbed and a song before he goes to sleep.
- Music has a tremendous effect on children and soft music and slower activities can be used to send out signals that it is time to sleep just as the smell of dinner tells a baby food is on the way.
- Some babies develop the need to have transitional comfort objects, such as cloths or a toy. This is their need at that time and should be respected. Look at the babies' sleep area very carefully.

Toddlers

Toddlers are movers and shakers and tend not to want to stop and rest. Some do need a short nap after lunch and so once lunch has finished start winding them down. In day care they may sleep on floor mattresses and need to have space between them in an area that can be darkened if possible. Good, consistent routines by all staff are vital. Because toddlers are all unique and their night sleep patterns vary, amounting to an average of 10 hours' sleep, it follows that their daytime afternoon naps, although offered, may not be needed. This presents a need to be flexible for those toddlers who will not sleep. They will need to be given a quiet activity or just allowed to rest with a favourite soft toy.

Practical activities

- Role play is how children learn. Providing beds (boxes) for teddies and dollies with little pillows and blankets encourages children to reflect and imitate the rules that you have implemented. Even having a teddy/dolly bed near their mattress and allowing a ritual of putting teddy/dolly to bed and then going to bed themselves can help. This is a wonderful time to observe their behaviour.

- Playing music helps to set the scene with toddlers, and whispering and using lowered tones reinforces sleep time behaviour. The tracks chosen need to be slow in tempo and rhythm. Cool down/calm down times are important.

- Choosing stories that have illustrations of going to bed help too. Talking and pointing to the pictures starts to get toddlers to talk about sleep time and understand the boundaries and rules that go with this time. Talking to parents to find out sleep time rituals and what happens at home helps carers to understand some of the patterns of behaviour a child displays when attending a day care setting.

- Everyone needs time for rest and maybe not actual sleeping. An area or zone with soft furnishings and perhaps a basket of soft toys or books, allows children time out from the busy activity that goes on in a toddler room.

Outcomes for the child

- Sleep nourishes and rest enables activity later.
- A burst of concentration will often follow sleep. Before sleep, babies and toddlers signal and get tearful as they grow weary.
- Rest and play starts to form sequences in a day.

Focus points

Toddlers have spurts of energy, these do not synchronise when they come into a group. Some children need to have some personal space and time to reflect and assimilate and if it is available they will use it. Alternatively rest time gives key workers an opportunity to build on their relationship with the children and share a cuddle or a book together

Caution: Ensuring that all safety regulations for correct and safe sleeping are met requires vigilance. Make sure that procedures are in place to check sleep patterns and that sleep positions are safe.

Staff discussion

It is important to ensure that sleep areas are appropriate. Highly over-decorated rooms do not support sleeping for young children.

- Is your sleep room conducive to sleep and relaxation? Think about the sleep room just as much as any other area such as an activity room. Ensure it is a sleep area not a storage area for unused items. Rooms with busy décor will not encourage young children to sleep.

- Are all staff aware of the standards required for sleep rooms and do they follow them every day?

⚠ **Caution:** Cot deaths have made parents more vigilant. Policies must always be followed and any concerns immediately reported. Sleep monitors alone may not be adequate.

4. Supporting movement

Provide safe outdoor experiences which challenge and support the development of both large and small movements

(*Birth to Three Matters*)

Babies

Aim to take babies outside every day. Wrap them up well against the weather and allow them to experience the fresh air, wind, sun and rain.

Practical activities

- Fix stimulating items outdoors wherever you can, such as colourful streamers, spinning CDs, balloons, wind-socks, flags or mobiles. Hold the baby safely and point to the items then move closer so the baby can reach out and touch them.

- Introduce items that make a sound so the baby turns her head to look for them. Look in garden centres for ornamental butterflies and birds. Buy two of each and put one outside and one inside at baby's eye level. Teach the finger rhyme 'Two little dickie birds sitting on a wall, one named Peter one named Paul. Fly away Peter, fly away Paul. Come back Peter, come back Paul' and use appropriate gestures.

- Make a simple hammock from a blanket. Lie the blanket on the ground and place the baby on her back on the blanket. With a colleague take the ends and gently swing the blanket to and fro. Sing 'Rock-a-bye baby'. Hold baby safely and swing high then low.

- Try 'Peek-a-boo' in pairs. Two adults, each holding a baby carefully, swing the babies towards each other so that they can look at each other and then away. Repeat this action. Alternatively perform this in front of a mirror so that the baby can see her own reflection.

- Once the baby has reached the crawling stage provide short tunnels or open-ended cardboard boxes for her to wriggle her way through. Place a toy at the other side and encourage her to reach it. Try this inside and outside.

Toddlers

Toddlers will need time to develop larger movements such as running. It requires both balance and co-ordination and to begin with they may stumble or fall over. Ensure there is a supportive adult close by to encourage their efforts.

Practical activities

- A pushchair can provide a toddler with additional support and walking confidence. Take the dolls for a stroll outside, imitating Mummy going shopping. Provide items for them to collect along the way.

- Mark out footstep shapes to follow along a path to help co-ordination.

- Act out stories such as 'I am going on a bear hunt' or 'Follow my leader', with the toddlers watching and imitating your movements. Encourage the toddler to use all his body as he crawls and growls. Try a range of animal actions, for example an elephant stamping, a pony trotting or a frog hopping.

- Throwing and catching encourages gross motor skills and hand–eye co-ordination. Use a washing basket and balls; try to get the ball into the basket. Vary the size of the balls, the distance from the basket and the size of the basket to increase the skill of this activity.

- Teach the song 'Five little speckled frogs'. Make a pond from a large cardboard shape and fix it securely to the ground so that it doesn't move on contact. From a secure launching pad, such as a stable block or stool, encourage the toddler to be a frog and to jump into the 'pond'. Extend this activity by making the pond smaller, further away or increasing the height of the launching pad. This will help to develop balance and co-ordination.

- Explore yoga for infants to help to develop and strengthen their growing bodies (see 'Resources'). It also helps them to relax and focus.

Outcomes for the child

- Spatial awareness and concept of self in space.
- Exploration and curiosity.
- Strengthening and developing large muscles.
- Independence and confidence.
- Balance and co-ordination.

Focus points

Every time a baby moves she is using and testing her developing muscles and getting stronger. She may need to be motivated to move so put interesting objects or toys just out of reach so she has to stretch. She will also be learning how to follow her gaze and gesture.

Check how the baby crawls: using one arm and its opposite leg then the other arm and its opposite leg. Crawling will help to develop bilateral movement skills which activate both sides of the brain in harmony. This is necessary for the development of the basic skills for reading and communication, the visual and speech and language centres.

Caution: Take into consideration the requirements of the Day Care Standards 4 and 6 (DfES/DWP, 2003) for the outside area. Toddlers may not yet have developed controlled balance so watch them carefully around steps and stairs.

Staff discussion

Toddlers aged 2–3 years are a boundless source of energy but get tired quickly.

● Do you observe the times of the day when they are most active and organise activities appropriately?

5. Gaining control of the body

Children only gradually gain control of their whole bodies
(Birth to Three Matters)

 Babies

By six months babies are aware that their hands are connected to their arms and they are developing good control. They are ready to explore their environment by reaching out and grabbing. Under six months most babies are not ready to use their thumbs to grasp and may need to use both their hands to hold a bottle and may drop it.

Practical activities

● A small plastic spice bottle is large enough for a baby to wrap her hands around and pull nearer for closer inspection. Half fill a plastic bottle with items that will stimulate her interest both visually and aurally. Look for objects that will create a sound: dried beans, sand, buttons, pasta shapes, pebbles or shells. Shake the bottle to gain her attention and to demonstrate the sound of the contents; lift the bottle to your ear and ask 'What is that?' Let her experiment freely.

- Provide a visual experience. Cut sparkly wrapping paper into strips and place inside the bottle or use glitter, coloured confetti or brightly coloured ribbons.

- Introduce a pleasant sensory experience with a simply squeeze and smell action. Sports bottles, those that have a pop-up top, can be filled with different smells and when squeezed release the aroma. Sprinkle a few drops of lavender oil or vanilla onto cotton wool and place in the bottle. Secure the top. Show how when the bottle is squeezed the aroma is puffed out via the flip top.

> **Caution:** Be aware that some smells are quite strong and could irritate a baby's nostrils or make her eyes water.

Toddlers

Toddlers develop control at their own individual rate. The child needs to gain competence at each stage in order to acquire a skill. Progress may appear slow in some areas and rapid in others. A variation in growth and development between toddlers is normal.

Practical activities

- Using liquids inside a bottle requires control and careful manipulation as the weight and balance changes when the liquid moves. Mix cooking oil with water and food colouring, and as the bottle is handled the contents will swirl and change. The effects can be increased by adding coloured lamp oil.

- Paint brightly coloured geometric designs onto a plastic bottle and add some weight by half filling it with marbles. As it rolls, the design will twist and turn and the marbles will move. Sit facing a toddler and roll the bottle towards him. Encourage him to push it back and forth. Experiment with the different effects caused by putting in fewer marbles or almost filling the bottle.

> **Caution:** Check that you use non-toxic paint.

- Fill plastic bottles with ready-mix paint; show how to squeeze the bottle to expel the paint and create a picture. Select the bottle carefully; too large a bottle and too hard a plastic will be difficult for a young child to manipulate. Swirl two colours together and encourage them to use their hands to mix them together.

- Half fill a bottle with small nails, pins and a variety of metal objects. Seal the top securely. Use a magnet on the outside to move the metal objects around inside the bottle. Extend this by including non-metallic objects and ask an open question such as 'I wonder why the paper has not moved?

Outcomes for the child

- Developing hand–eye co-ordination.
- Developing manipulation using fine and gross motor skills and strengthening and developing muscles.

Focus points

Children develop their muscles from the top down and from the inside outside: head–core–legs–hands and then feet. In order to develop these muscles they need good nutrition as it requires a great deal of energy. These developing muscles also need exercise and practice.

Ask parents and staff to collect plastic bottles and tops. Look for different shapes, sizes, colours and weight.

Caution: Always have bottled water available as exercise may cause dehydration. Offer water regularly. Be aware of the factors that affect children's need for water, these include heat, energetic games, illness and some medication. Encourage children to ask for a drink.

Staff discussion

- Get staff together and create a wide range of interesting bottles.
- Could you encourage parents and staff to collect plastic bottles and tops? Ask them to look for different shapes, sizes, colours and weight. They will need to have been washed thoroughly and dried before use. Seal contents with strong tape or a low-temperature glue gun.
- Could you connect the contents to planned themes, such as an autumn bottle, mini beasts or a single colour?
- Do you encourage children to create things at home and bring them to the setting to talk about?

6. Acquiring physical skills

Make opportunities for young children to feed themselves using fingers, forks and spoons

(*Birth to Three Matters*)

Babies

A baby may be able to sit up at around six months and take an interest in her surroundings. Then as her trunk becomes stronger she will gain better control of her arms and hands.

Practical activities

- Encourage babies to take control of their feeding bottle by gently holding it with them and gradually removing your support until they can begin to feed themselves. Maintain eye contact, smile and use soft words as they feed.

- Initially babies need full fat food for energy, but later on try to provide a variety of textures such as creamy mashed potatoes, soft cheese, scrambled eggs or stewed fruit. Hold a small spoonful up to your nose and say 'Yum yum'. Encourage the baby to smell the food and offer her a spoonful at a time, placed on the tip of her tongue. Watch how she responds; if she spits it out or turns her head, leave it and try again another time.

> ⚠ **Caution:** Always confer with parents over a child's diet or possible cultural aspects of food. Some may use their fingers rather than cutlery.

35

- Put some cooked peas on a tray in front of the baby and show her how to pick them up and feed herself. Allow her to play with food on a tray, making traces and swirls. Introduce couscous or oats and encourage her to squeeze it through her fingers and experience the texture. This may be messy but it can be fun and strengthens the wrists and fingers.

> ⚠️ **Caution:** Be aware of contact allergies.

- To further develop these muscles set up two or three metal pots and wooden spoons. Show her how to hold the spoon and bang the drum to make a noise. Note: plastic bowls are quieter.

Toddlers

Provide a range of activities so that toddlers can acquire the necessary practice in the skills they need to use everyday tools such as spoons, forks and knives.

Practical activities

- Provide a range of large and small mixing bowls, cereal bowls and soup bowls together with different shapes and sizes of spoons. Include wooden spoons, serving spoons and serving tongs. Fill the bowls with dried fruit, cereal and pasta shapes. Let the children stir the food, play with it and transfer from one bowl to another. When necessary show them how to hold the spoons correctly.

- Introduce different textures such as cold cooked spaghetti, mashed-up banana and dried peas.

- Develop this activity into simple cooking techniques that require combining ingredients by stirring and mixing.

- Help them to make their own play dough.

- Set up a tea party role-play situation with dolls, or teddy bears. Have bibs, spoons and a selection of dried food. Play alongside, feeding the dolls.

- Try stirring and spooning different textures such as sawdust or lentils, or fill a bowl with ice-cubes and let the toddler stir them around, gradually melting the ice. In winter time fill a bowl with snow.

> ⚠️ **Caution:** Be rigorous about cleaning up spilt food so as not to encourage vermin or ants etc.

Outcomes for the child

- Developing hand–eye co-ordination.
- Manipulation using fine and gross motor skills.
- Developing independence and confidence.

Focus points

A baby's first sensory experience is through her mouth. Motor skills develop gradually as children learn to gain control over their bodies and many everyday activities can be effectively used to encourage these skills. From an early age they want to be independent and are keen to do things for themselves. Helping them to use everyday tools competently will enable them to feed themselves. At around two years she should be able to feed herself but at times may be quite messy.

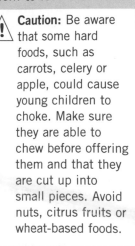

Caution: Be aware that some hard foods, such as carrots, celery or apple, could cause young children to choke. Make sure they are able to chew before offering them and that they are cut up into small pieces. Avoid nuts, citrus fruits or wheat-based foods.

An important aspect when it comes to feeding is supporting children to have control over what and how much they eat. Hunger signals vary from child to child: they may cry, chew their fist or open their mouths wide; some may become irritable. Watch for the signs that a baby uses to tell you she is full: does she turn her head, dribble food from her mouth or slow down? Don't pressurise a child to eat or insist she eats certain things. Children know when they are full or hungry and what appeals to them.

Staff discussion

- Do you observe and record the babies' hunger signals?
- Is the eating area an attractive environment? Display photos of children, food, cutlery, family meals.
- Do staff eat and talk with the children? Young children learn by copying and imitating adults.

References

DfES (Department for Education and Skills) (2002) *Birth to Three Matters: A Framework to Support Children in their Earliest Years.* London: DfES.

DfES (Department for Education and Skills) (2003) *Every Child Matters.* London: DfES.

Ofsted (Office for Standards in Education)/DfES (Department for Education and Skills) (2003) *Full Day Care: Guidance to the National Standards.* London: DfES.

Resources

Child, L. (2001) *I Will Never, Not Ever, Eat a Tomato.* London: Orchard Books.

Cooper, H. (1999) *Pumpkin Soup.* New York: Farrar Straus Giroux.

Dennison, P. (1992) *Brain Gym.* Ventura, CA: Edu-Kinesthetics Inc.

Ehlert, L. (1996) *Eating the Alphabet.* Orlando, FL: Red Wagon Books.

Levenson, G. (2002) *Pumpkin Circle: The Story of a Garden.* Berkeley, CA: Ten Speed Press.

Sharmat, M. (1984) *Gregory the Terrible Eater.* New York: Scholastic.

Watanabe, S. (1982) *How do I Eat It?* London: Random House.

Whiting, M. (2001) *Managing Nursery Food.* London: Orchard Books.

For advice on diet and health visit the Food Standards Agency website – www.food.gov.uk

Natural food colourings can be bought from Overseal Natural Ingredients – www.overseal.co.uk

For further information about Body Balance Books, phone 020 8202 9747.

A range of soft bird toys with authentic bird songs can be obtained from the RSPB – www.rspb.org.uk/

Further advice on yoga for infants can be found on the British Wheel of Yoga website (www.bwy.org.uk) or by phoning 01529 306851 and from Yoga Bugs (www.yogabugs.com) tel. 020 8772 1800.

3 Keeping safe

Introduction

Babies and toddlers are vulnerable and rely on responsible adults to care for them. Human babies unlike animals cannot stand, move around and feed themselves from birth. They need to be kept safe in terms of their physical well-being but also their social and emotional well-being. Feeling safe means they can relax and enjoy exploring their world, growing in independence, skills and knowledge. This feeds their self-esteem.

Regulations have become much more specific since the mid-1990s. Ofsted enforces safety regulations on childminders and settings, requiring standards to be met every day. Parents are more aware of safety issues too, because in the workplace, regulations are open and accessible to all. Safety regulations and literature relating to equipment and toys is publicised and labels have to be specific and conform with standards laid down in EC law.

Food safety is now a huge issue and the media quickly informs the general public when there are concerns about the safety of particular products. Baby and toddler allergies are on the increase and should be at the forefront of any carer's mind. *Every Child Matters* is a government strategy in which Staying Safe is identified as the second key area in the framework. This illustrates the fact that everyone should take responsibility for providing safe environments for children and ensuring that they have security and stability and are properly cared for.

In this chapter the focus is on ensuring that babies and toddlers are safe and protected. In order to do this we need to look at boundaries, limits, asking for help, learning when to say no and anticipating when others will do so.

1. Staying safe

For young children, provide different arrangements of toys and soft play materials to encourage crawling, hiding and peeping

(*Birth to Three Matters*)

Babies

Young babies make purposeful movements and tend not to stay in the positions they are placed. Placing babies on their tummy develops and strengthens their muscles and encourages positive brain developments. It is important to ensure they are on a safe surface and free from any possible risks such as open doorways/pathways.

Practical activities

- Whatever their age, young children need to be stimulated, and so when they lie on their tummy ensure that they can see and reach their favourite toy. Adults interacting with the baby must also be prepared to lie down so they can make eye contact and use gestures and voice tone to communicate effectively.

- A baby who is laid on her tummy has a vision of 9 inches from the floor. Bear this in mind when placing her favourite toy within her eye range level and reach so the whole of the toy can be focused upon.

● Early crawlers need a safe surface. Children need a safe grip to launch their feet from. Plastic tiles or laminate flooring can prove slippery and do not allow their toes to grip well. By purchasing two or three bath mats (and fixing them together to create a mini pathway) you can provide a safe surface and texture, which they can grip in their bare feet. Inevitably babies dribble or are sick on these and they can be easily cleaned which means they are safe and hygienic.

Toddlers

Toddlers need opportunities to practise their walking, toddling, climbing and running and build up a sense of danger. Toddler areas therefore need to be carefully planned in terms of their layout. Often they appear too sparse which can increase risks by encouraging haphazard running as well as providing a less stimulating environment with little real challenge. If they are too crowded and cluttered, however, it does not allow fluid movement opportunities.

Practical activities

● Set up simple obstacle challenges such as several large plastic cola/lemonade bottles filled with liquids or pebbles. Place at regular intervals to encourage the children to move safely between obstacles. This can be extended by encouraging them to take a teddy for a walk or push a buggy in and out of them.

● Using short tunnels to crawl through builds up confidence of being in an enclosed/enveloped space. Pop-up laundry baskets, with the ends cut out, provide small tunnels.

● Use literacy as a starting point, for example Little Red Riding Hood and her journey to see her grandma. Plant three small conifer bushes in pots and space them out before drawing a chalk pathway that goes in and out of the trees to represent the journey through the wood/forest. Ask toddlers to travel on a wheeled vehicle to Grandma's house or to walk along the path to Grandma's.

● Set up 'roundabouts' using soft play equipment, boxes, or tyres so that children can experience moving in a circular route. This encourages children to use their left and right body movements that link up with and develop both sides of the brain.

Outcomes for the child

- Building up an inner sense of 'keeping safe'.
- Sensing dangers – yet encouraging a sense of curiosity and exploration.
- Knowing when and how to ask for help – supporting a sense of personal well-being.
- Beginning to appreciate simple rules for moving safely.

Focus points

Observe how children begin to develop their sense of safety as they grow. For example, when a team of carers work with babies on the correct way to crawl, march and climb, babies will gain confidence and skill.

Encourage staff to find out from parents what they are currently trying to get across to their children in terms of safety – so you could work on these together.

Staff discussion

- Do staff get together and decide on a rota to ensure that the outside space is checked daily?
- Are staff encouraged to find out from parents what they are doing to help their children learn about safety? Can you find ways to work together on this?
- Work on one important concept for very young children such as 'Hot'. Take photos of times when children need to be kept safe, for example if the dinner is hot, blowing on it to cool it.
- If equipment is unsafe, do all staff know what to do with it? If something is removed from the equipment, how soon will it be replaced and by whom?

2. Games we can play

**Given opportunities to practise what they can do in safe surroundings,
young children learn some sense of danger**

(Birth to Three Matters)

Babies

Babies have opportunities to explore the sense of danger through play. Good interactions with their key person help them to experience and learn many new things. By allowing the play to be open ended their imagination grows as they play with everyday objects. They can begin to experience new emotions in a safe environment when they play a simple game of 'Peepo'. This game enables them to see that the adult has not actually left them, merely been hidden from view for a brief moment.

Practical activities

- Using very soft see-through scarves and teddies play 'Peepo'. Gradually hide the teddies for longer periods. Later extend this activity by using puppets.
- Use tubes or coloured plastic pet tubes (short hamster tunnels) and pull soft scarves through and pull away. The scarves pass easily through the tubes.
- Use your hands and face to hide from and peep at the baby – in their early stages of development children love looking at faces.
- Hide bright balls under cloths and lift them to show babies they are there. Say 'Peepo' when doing this.
- Hide toys under boxes and encourage crawlers to find them – keep lifting the box up to reassure the baby that the toy is still safe and has not disappeared.

Toddlers

Using games as a way of thinking about safety is ideal. Toddlers start to understand that there are people who help to keep us safe, for example the police, fire and hospital staff. Playing in a home corner with house equipment also presents an opportunity to look at a healthy, safe environment and to consider risks – understanding that an oven is hot, doors that are shut quickly may hurt you if you are not careful, etc. Running when carrying things and not looking where you are going can be a hazard even when you are playing.

Practical activities

- Look at Jack in the boxes – they are safe in their box but pop up. When we get up we need to look around. Practise bobbing up and down to music.
- Move in a circle holding hands and explain that moving safely means watching others and not bumping into or hurting them.
- Use pieces of material, for example scarves or saris, to start simple parachute play experiences. Start by doing this sitting down in groups of four or in a pair. Put a soft ball on top of the material and flip it up in the air. Because all the equipment is soft it is safe.
- Children do have accidents. Allow them to talk about accidents and have a collection of board books which focus on this. Some of the books may have stories with nurses and doctors.
- Climbing up and down – encourage children to climb up, ensuring they have the correct footwear and clothing on and that surfaces are stable. This can be linked to well-loved stories such as 'Jack and the Beanstalk'.

Outcomes for the child

- Gaining a sense of danger.
- Taking risks within a safe environment.
- Being able to ask for help and support for physical challenges that are faced.

Focus points

It is important to understand that some children sense danger early and use their experiences to debate what risks they will take. Some children do not enjoy risks and the feeling of danger really impacts on their well-being. Bad experiences stop them from trying new experiences for a while; the next time they face a similar situation they may need a sensitive adult to get them over an initial feeling of fear.

Staff discussion

- Discuss individual children and how they cope with situations where they feel in danger such as early walkers who wobble and feel unsure. How can we support them and remove that sense of danger?
- Could staff discretely collect photos of when children fall over and how they are comforted and put them together to form an 'Ouch' book? This is a book which could stimulate discussions with toddlers.

3. Moving safely

Beginning to walk, climb and run with little sense of danger, babies focus on what they *want*

(Birth to Three Matters)

Babies

Once babies move off their tummy their view of the world is extended to approximately 21 inches. Pulling up their body and beginning to walk is a tremendous achievement. They start to become explorers; however, they are not experienced in this new world and are not always aware of their limits.

Practical activities

● When babies begin to be ready for walking hold them firmly under their arms and sing or say a simple rhyme such as:

> *Up and down we go (say twice)*
> *You and me*
> *High and low*
> *Up and down we go*

Positive reactions such as a smile and firm support give a feeling of being safe.

● Using a simple, traditional push-along toy with an appropriate height handle allows those just standing to have a support to use while they develop their confidence levels. Ensure that the toy has a clear area to be moved in and remember to praise the child when he achieves even a short distance at first.

● Up and down movements encourage muscle development. Use simple, transparent scarves, throwing them up and letting them fall. Ensure that the object that is being thrown is safe and soft and can do no harm even if it lands on a head or face.

Toddlers

Toddlerhood means that many 'firsts' happen and so this is a time for learning about danger. Risks can be eliminated if appropriate toys are used and space is well thought out. Use simple, clear commands such as 'No!' and explaining that they may get hurt. Role play, stories and rhymes play their part in getting the message across.

● Jack and Jill went up the hill – ask children to hold hands with a friend (replace their names instead of Jack and Jill) and let them march to the top of the hill and fall down and roll down the hill. Give them lots of space between the pairs so that they can do the actions, or let them demonstrate one pair at a time while the others watch. Let them use small, soft plastic buckets and talk and point to see where they went as they fell.

● Very simple obstacle walking trails encourage children to avoid objects in their path. Simply use brightly coloured picnic plates so they can see them and negotiate them easily.

● Use simple baby blankets or thin net cloths with a soft toy on them to transport a toy or as a parachute to encourage movement and carrying skills.

● Practise carrying pretend food on a plate, moving safely as part of role play. This will get across the need to walk slowly sometimes for safety reasons.

Outcomes for the child

- Greater understanding that moving can have elements of danger that need to be appreciated.
- Developing new skills for running, balancing and climbing.
- Appreciating that others need space too.

Focus points

There is a fine balance between keeping safe and over-protecting young children. Ensure that worry about being safe does not affect them so much that they are anxious about trying out new experiences. Focus on different strategies to get attention and warn children that they are in danger without frightening them and causing an accident, for example using sounds or breaks in music as a signal to stop. Teaching them control and stopping them when they are walking and running too fast is a good way to raise aware of speed, control and safety.

Staff discussion

- Do staff discuss health and safety relating to the building, remembering the garden area if there is one?
- Have the team worked on one aspect, for example climbing, encouraging babies to climb over cushions and toddlers to climb over and under items? Consider the level of interaction and intervention that might be needed.

4. Safe choices

Provide opportunities for babies and children to have choices in an environment kept safe by knowledgeable adults who know there should be a balance between freedom and safe limits

(Birth to Three Matters)

Babies

Babies can be offered simple choices in their play and options in relation to food once they start to feed on solid foods. Choices help them grow in terms of their independence and interdependence.

Practical activities

- Place young babies in activity rings and offer them a choice of different balls (all checked for size and safety with a young baby) such as woven or plastic open balls, fresh unwaxed fruit, soft material balls. Offer and show them one by one so they see there is choice and watch them choosing.

- Place a seated baby on a soft rug surface and present her with a collection of rattles. If she is teething, provide soothing rattles that can be sucked safely. Babies tend to put things in their mouth immediately. Offer two or three different rattles; there are many designs on the market at the moment but you should ensure they have the EC quality standards mark on the label.

- Be aware that placing babies in rockers, car seats and buggies for long periods of time is neither safe nor healthy and babies have no choices regarding this. Knowledgeable adults must be aware of the length of time that babies are restrained and allow them some freedom in safe limits.

Toddlers

The addition of mobility in toddlerhood can present adults with additional challenges. Planning for free times when toddlers can direct their own play and times when they work in a small group or with a key worker is important. Within free time activities toddlers will find opportunities that may lead to unsafe play. Once something has occurred it is important that toddlers are calmly told of the dangers of what they have done and reminded when they return to the activity of what happened before.

Practical activities

- When offering play dough ensure that cutters are not sharp and any food colouring used does not contain additives. When cooking dough use herbal tea bags, such as cranberry and raspberry, to impart colour, texture and aroma safely.

- For painting consider using sponge scrubbers with reservoirs that are for washing up. Filling these with paint means that children are less likely to spill paint or water and won't lose the focus on the painting by worrying about parents being cross about dirty clothes.

- Outside have arrow symbols on the plastic climbing frames to show which way you are to go up to avoid conflict and accidents.

Outcomes for the child

- Children can focus on a task if they feel they can have some freedom but will refer to an adult in a positive way if they are unsure.

- Children learn from their mistakes and become more aware if safety is pointed out in a constructive way.

- Children start to see safety is necessary within play.

Focus points

The changing world presents different perceptions of what keeping safe may mean and it is influenced by our experiences. Children who are over-protected can miss out on excitement or challenge. Finding out about how parents deal with the issue of safety gives an insight into how the child feels about keeping safe.

Staff discussion

- Do staff talk about what they are doing when they put down crash mats or test the water temperature to make sure it is not too hot? They need to balance their tone and pace, asking or telling the children why they are doing this.

- Talk together about the stories and songs we use that may help children to understand safety, for example 'Humpty Dumpty'.

- Discuss safety routines in the setting, for example at lunchtime when the rice pudding is hot what do we do?

- Talk about outside play and how we keep the environment safe. When was the sand tray last cleaned? When was the equipment checked for safety?

5. Knowing when and how to ask for help

Note the ways in which babies indicate what they need, including help from the adults

(*Birth to Three Matters*)

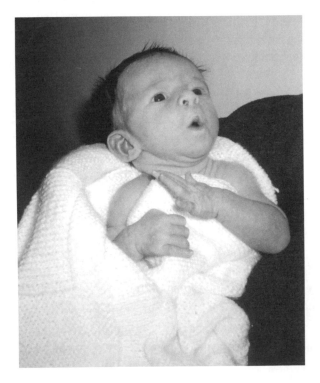

Babies

Babies do not have language but they have many other ways of letting us know what they want and when they want it! They use sounds and gestures and body language to get across what they are feeling and needing at different points in the day. Something as simple as rubbing behind their ears and moving their heads may signal they are tired and need sleep.

Practical activities

- Collect photographs of the signals babies use and what they are telling us. For example, closing their lips tightly and shaking the heads to say 'no more'.

- Listen to a baby crying and the pitches she uses – is she in distress or attempting to get attention from an adult? Make a note of when crying is used to indicate needs.

- Babies sometimes reach out to indicate need. Provide activities that encourage this reaching out, such as baby gyms or mobiles they can touch, to encourage stretching and grasping.

- Consider 'Baby signing' as another method of communication. Baby Signing is the use of gestures as a form of communication with babies before they begin to speak. It can be used alongside the spoken word, or without. For example, the sign for 'milk' is represented as a tilting movement using an imaginary bottle. It is more graphic than British Sign Language. Use this alongside the adult speaking to the baby.

- Only mirror the positive signs and gestures babies make. Avoid imitating negative cries.

Toddlers

Once language has developed toddlers use very simplistic orders or instructions to get across their needs such as 'me wants that' or 'that's mine'. They try language but often use physical actions to get what they need. A climate of 'it's good to ask for help' needs to be developed. The key person may verbally encourage a child by reminding him to ask for help when it is really needed.

Practical activities

- Use role play such as shop play where adults are actively involved and provide good role models.

- When it is lunchtime ask who needs help to cut up their food. Look at routines and offer help; observe and intervene when you see that a toddler is getting frustrated or upset.

- Encourage children to help each other and say 'thank you' afterwards. When a child is sad and needs a tissue ask another child to get the tissue box. This makes him feel part of helping someone else.

- Within the day ask 'Who will help me – to water the plants, hand out the biscuits?' and so on. This gives the message that we all need help at times and it is OK to ask for help.

Outcomes for the child

- Communicating your needs ensures that you get help and support and you are feeling safe.
- Understanding others can help you.
- Asking for help can bring about safety, closeness and understanding.

Focus points

Babies have their own preferences and they can make their needs known. Some of these signs can be very individual and key workers/carers need to identify these and share them so that everyone appreciates the babies' individual signs and signals and the response is consistent.

There are people whose job is to help us out of dangerous situations (fire people, doctors, etc.) and whom we can ask for help. Role playing this helps toddlers to understand what they do.

Staff discussion

- Check that all staff have opportunities to practise fire alarm procedure at different times of the day – check the safety of every child throughout this. What contingency plans are in place and how does everyone know them?

- Look at the safety record and see when accidents have occurred. Is it when children have not asked for help and tried to do things themselves? Discuss this.

- Are there any children who rarely ask for help? Discuss why this is.

6. Keeping safe

Being safe and protected includes discovering boundaries and limits
(Birth to Three Matters)

Babies

Babies start to follow simple trails and understand simple boundaries. After birth their vision develops from being black and white to colour. Giving simple, secure boundaries such as lying in a Moses basket or a cot makes them feel safe. However, later they need to develop a sense of a wider world. They become aware of their own space around their bodies. Simple play gym frames ensure babies can see and touch items hung above them and get a sense of the boundary in space above their heads.

Practical activities

- Make or print off simple pictures for babies and laminate them – place them on the floor securely and encourage the baby to move from one to another. This is making a trail and provides early boundaries.

- Put some plastic bottles filled with coloured water on some place mats to encourage the baby to crawl or move from one to another in a vertical line or in a circle which is a boundary.

- Make a horizontal trail. Use a curtain pole with items attached such as keys, rattles, wooden spoons. Fix this securely to the wall at a low level. It presents a treasure trail for the baby to explore.

- Place toys onto soft mats and arrange the mats so that the babies are a safe distance from one another.

Toddlers

Toddlers still need physical boundaries, but as their speech develops the carer or practitioner has another strategy to call upon when thinking about boundaries. A boundary sets the limits on behaviour. Most boundaries concentrate on keeping children safe, for example 'we never slam doors'.

Practical activities

- Use simple, clear language when asking children to do things and support the action needed. Follow it up and make it possible for them to carry out your instructions. For example, use see-through boxes with pictures on so that when you say tidy up, the toddlers will know where things go and can see how the rule is possible.

- Use stories that have boundaries in them such as *Rosie's Walk* by Pat Hutchins. This story is set in a farmyard area – it has a boundary.

- Start to establish a cosy zone – which has soft furnishings with cushions and soft toys. This will establish the idea of an area set aside for a specific purpose with clear boundaries.

- Use a carpet runner for cars and wheeled toys to be pushed along. This is a pathway for play and another example of a boundary.

- Outside areas need clear boundaries for a dedicated Bike Park so that it is a safe bike zone for children to play in.

Outcomes for the child

- Being aware of an area or zone as a place in which to play.
- Playing in a special place with specific equipment supports safe play.
- Being safe means being aware of others near or in your space.

Focus points

Boundaries and limits mean that there need to be some physical signs or collections of items such as cork board mats, soft washable mats and bamboo mats. These provide choice, diversity and impact on a child's space.

Staff discussion

- What resources do we have to support the physical environment in terms of boundaries and limits?
- How long are babies kept in unnecessary boundaries – cots, buggies and bouncers – each day?
- Can we make some positive changes to this by being mindful at tummy time and during unrestricted floor play?
- Discuss what boundaries we have outside apart from the outer boundaries. How can boundaries outside be achieved?

References

DfES (Department for Education and Skills) (2002) *Birth to Three Matters: A Framework to Support Children in their Earliest Years.* London: DfES.

DfES (Department for Education and Skills) (2003) *Every Child Matters.* London: DfES.

Ofsted (Office for Standards in Education)/DfES (Department for Education and Skills) (2003) *Full Day Care: Guidance to the National Standards.* London: DfES.

Resources

Hutchins, P. (1968) *Rosie's Walk.* USA: Simon & Schuster.

Signs for Success – www.signsforsuccess.co.uk

4 | Healthy choices

Introduction

Can we offer young children real and genuine choices? Can we respect their choice and support it? Children are individuals; they do not all have the same needs, abilities, expectations, skills or experience. If they are able to make a choice and are supported in following their own interests, they are more motivated and involved in the learning process.

For a child to make a choice he needs to be able to consider a number of realistic alternatives. He has to become familiar with them in order to make a considered decision not a random choice. Children need to be given opportunities and time to explore, to try out resources, situations, friendships, and then have the freedom to make a mistake, before they make a decision. They become empowered and learn why they want something and what they want to do with it. This is an integral part of the High/Scope philosophy (Hohmann and Weikart, 2002). It has been used by the authors since 1962 and encourages adults and children to share control of the learning experiences.

The Effective Early Learning (EEL) project (Pascal and Bertram, 1997) uses observations of children's involvement and autonomy to evaluate the quality of learning in a setting. The researchers have formulated a set of criteria to assess what the children are doing and to form these judgements. Periods of free choice give the practitioner an ideal opportunity to observe the pace, the level of interest and the development of a child's skills.

1. Making choices

Infants and toddlers in group care have no choice about being in childcare. Each part of the day, however, presents opportunities for choices and decisions they can make. Making these choices on a daily basis and being able to change their minds from one day to the next tends to give children a sense of control over their day

(Birth to Three Matters)

 Babies

Young babies may be immobile and without language, but they can be offered choices and can make their choice known. Given the choice of sweet or sour they will opt for sweet items as their sense of taste is prone to sweetness in the early stages of their development illustrating that some of the choices they make relate to specific developments. An obvious strategy they use when they choose to say 'I do not want any more food' is to pull away and move their head from side to side or keep their lips firmly together. This signals 'enough'. Starting to build up simple choices means limited choice – using two items.

Practical activities

Here are some simple examples that can be used. Setting these exercises up several times will build up a pattern which will inform you of general likes and dislikes.

● Food choices – place two items of food on a baby plate or clean highchair tray and observe the response. Doing this daily and altering the choice will add and offer choice to the baby.

- In a small wicker basket place two rattles and show the baby how she can access them – taking them in and out and rattling them. Observe if she chooses a specific rattle every time.

- Later using a treasure basket introduce a collection of items made from wood. Present this daily – does the baby choose the same item? Babies often focus on a favourite and if that is slightly hidden, they will search for it. Using simple containers with two compartments and physically splitting items is an aid to establishing choices, so you can offer them 'this or that'.

Toddlers

If children don't have a choice, they cannot make a decision. If they haven't experienced the items, they cannot make an informed choice. Many of the resources in a setting are new and unfamiliar to children and they don't know how to use them. They may use them in totally new and creative ways. As they explore the materials they will begin to discover more about their world, how things work, fit together or combine well with something else.

Practical activities

- Set up a cereal-making activity, with a variety of ingredients (raisins, oats, currants and so forth), a mixing bowl and spoons. Allow the children to sample each of the ingredients if they wish and to choose what to put into their mixing bowl. Encourage the children to talk about the choices they have made and why. Mix all the ingredients and eat at mealtime. This activity can be extended to sandwich making, soup or cake making.

> ⚠ **Caution:** Be aware of nut allergies.

- Provide a choice of snacks, selecting items that are similar but have different tastes, for example a slice of orange or a carrot, a stick of celery or a spring onion. Discuss what it is they like about the one they have chosen and extend their language – is it the colour, the taste, the texture.

- Always have a variety of mark-making tools available and encourage the children to choose which they wish to use. For example: a variety of papers, coloured and plain in different shapes and sizes; thick and thin pencils in colours and black; felt tip pens and chalk.

Outcomes for the child

- Choices help to establish likes and dislikes.
- Continual discovery about likes and dislikes.
- Children choose individually – recognition that choices are personal preferences.
- Children make discoveries about their world.

Focus points

When children are fully immersed in an activity high level learning is taking place. They are totally focused and oblivious to their surroundings. When they have completed an activity to their own satisfaction they may give a deep sigh. It is essential that adults respect children's choices and support them; in this way a child's self-worth is strengthened and he has confidence in his selection. The adult can talk to him about what he is going to do, and later ask him how it went.

Staff discussion

- Use observations to understand what strategies babies use to show their likes and dislikes, and share these with the team or parents. This will demonstrate that every child has a unique pattern of behaviour and is entitled to choices.
- Observe if the child is choosing according to a schema and support with appropriate materials. Remember: too many choices can overwhelm children but too few means no pace or progress and little opportunity to control their world.

2. Demonstrating individual preferences

Babies continually discover more about what they like and dislike
(Birth to Three Matters)

Babies

Babies all require the same level of care; however, they begin to demonstrate personal preferences as they mature. These preferences are built up through experiencing the world – 'their world'. This helps to develop an individual sense of self which is another component of *Birth to Three Matters* – A Strong Child.

'Demonstrating individual preferences' in this sense means that babies use their cries, gestures and body language to communicate their likes and dislikes.

Practical activities

- Listening carefully to the timbre of babies' cries is a useful indicator as to the levels of happiness and distress they are experiencing. Often when a new choice is introduced and there is a notable sense of dislike this can help you gauge the level of like or dislike.

- Babies signal their likes through facial expressions – note the look of glee on a baby's face as she enjoys some human interaction with a carer. Smiles, nonsense sounds and funny faces are important clues that can be indicators of preference.

- Body language is a key indicator of preference. If a baby withdraws her body it is signal of dislike and/or apprehension and when she reaches or is striving for more then she likes the food or toy she has interacted with.

Toddlers

During this stage a toddler is becoming self-assured, developing assertiveness which may be expressed through words and actions or by saying 'No'. They are spontaneous and moods can change quickly. As a toddler becomes aware of his likes and dislikes he may show a strong preference for his own style and how he presents himself to others.

Practical activities

- Make sure that resources are accessible, at the right height and can be safely reached.

- Notice what the children wear to the setting or the contents of their lunch boxes; find out if they choose freely for themselves. Observe if they show a preference for a favourite colour. Discuss with the children what they like/don't like about these things.

- During outdoor play observe which are the most favourite items. Do they all want to ride the red bike?

- Develop a stimulating role-play wardrobe where toddlers can try out different styles and be whoever they please. Let them wear the clothes throughout the day if they wish, indoors or outdoors.

- Extend the play so they can really imitate the adult world and pretend to do what adults do, for example by providing the extra resources for the young 'postie' to deliver letters and parcels.

- Have a selection of music that the children can choose from and play for themselves.

Outcomes for the child

- Becoming an individual – with individual preferences.
- Building up a sense of self – formed from experiences and making choices and preferences individual to them.
- Using non-verbal signals as a tool to communicate preferences to others.
- Developing self-confidence and self-assurance.

Focus points

Key workers or carers should have a good appreciation of every child's preferences. This knowledge will help them to make plans for new choices and appreciate any emotional support children will need. Investigate how this information is held and how information from parents is shared with regard to this.

It is essential that the adults listen to children and respect the children's choices and preferences. Through this the children are beginning to form their own individual personality and characteristics and the adult can begin to know and understand the unique qualities of each child.

Staff discussion

- How could you use information and communications technology (ICT) to capture a child's likes and dislikes?
- Are staff aware of the way in which individual children show their feelings?
- What evidence could you use to show that choices are part of the everyday programme offered to the children?
- What organisational changes might you have to make to allow children realistic choices?
- How can you show a child that you are really listening to him?

3. Taking control

From birth, babies show
preferences for people and
for what they want to see,
hear and taste
(*Birth to Three Matters*)

Babies

Most choices babies make are assisted by the touching or sucking of the item they wish to explore. The key sense post birth is touch. Babies need to discover their world and experience through touch using parts of their body to do so. Gentle and tentative exploratory touching may be part of the prerequisite to making a choice.

Babies may watch and stare at people in order to make a choice of who they wish to go to or appear most comfortable with. Discovering and learning about their bodies is important and using their senses to assist them to make choices starts early.

Here are some suggestions to try this out, using hands, feet and senses. Remember: results will vary depending on the child.

Practical activities

- Choose to experience materials – making handprints or footprints. The first time they feel paint on their hand they may not enjoy the sensation! Try using non-sensitive talcum powder and black paper to make a print. This may be an extension for some babies or a preferred experience for others because of the temperature and feel of the materials.

- Most early baby toys are made of materials that are safe for baby to grasp, such as towelling or soft terry cotton. Give baby two to choose from and observe the outcome.

- Babies' hands are very important – so are their feet. Tickle or touch them with two different items, for example a feather duster or the tips of your fingers. Observe their responses and note which they like best.

- Using two different sounds, one high and one low, watch a baby's response – which does she prefer?

Toddlers

During a session the toddlers experience different situations; some may be structured and planned by the practitioner while others allow the toddler to choose for themselves what they wish to play with and how they wish to use it. Often they will replicate activities undertaken with the practitioner, amending and developing them in their own way. Free choice time allows the practitioner the opportunity to observe how children learn and what they have understood.

Practical activities

- Provide a choice of wet or dry sand. Which do the children prefer?

- Follow a structured craft activity by allowing the children free choice with different materials. Notice what they do and how they use the materials. For example, create a collage with a variety of coloured paper, cellophane and shiny paper torn into shapes and glued. At another session remind them of what they made and introduce alongside the paper a choice of different fabrics, textures and shapes. How do the children respond? Which do they prefer? Do they use the paper as before or experiment with the new material?

- Allow the children to access a large cardboard box and a selection of smaller boxes and small world toys. Observe how they play.

- Use a story as a stimulus for free choice and supply resources to support and extend. For example, *Mrs Mopple's Washing Line* by Anita Hewett has a connecting schema. Have items of clothing, pegs, a laundry basket and a washing line where the toddler's can reach it.

Outcomes for the child

- Able to use their body language to show preferences and make choices.
- Taking control in a simple way and make decisions from the beginning if given opportunities and choices.

Focus points

Exploratory free choice time allows the practitioner the opportunity to observe how the child is developing and what he is learning. It is during these unstructured times that he explores materials, skills and ideas and later develops mastery. The practitioner can then plan structured play to take the learning further. Free play allows the practitioner to observe and identify schemas. Although babies' behaviour may appear to be accidental it is not always so. They may be operating a schema that the adult can support and extend.

Staff discussion

- Review your provision and consider the environment and the presentation of daily activities. Do staff recognise the benefits to the children if they have real choices within their day?

- Having this as a focus for a week and reviewing it afterwards may encourage staff to see they could add in more opportunities and step back from the daily routines that sometimes begin to dominate the days and weeks.

> ⚠ **Caution:** Make sure the balance is right in terms of choices and developmental stages. Too many choices too soon can be overwhelming.

4. Making decisions

Value and support the decisions children make and then go onto encourage them to try something else, recognising that one decision leads to another

(Birth to Three Matters)

 Babies

Making decisions is part of growing up. Learning how to consider what you will do rather than simply doing or saying something, is part of developing our own understanding of choices and decisions. For this reason it is essential that babies are provided with opportunities to practice these decision making skills in a safe environment as, at this stage, it is not the outcome of the decision which is of importance, rather it is the fact that the baby gets to make her own decision and gains a positive learning experience as a result.

Practical activities

- Place two pieces of fruit on a feeding chair or plate and let the baby choose which she wants first. It doesn't matter which one – she can eat either and she can have both.

- Roll two balls – perhaps of different textures or colours – and let her choose which one she will pick up first.

- Choosing when to have a drink – try a drink and if she rejects it, place it within eyesight so she can signal when she wants it. Repeat the offer or choice at regular intervals.

- Place two different tactile surfaces on either side of a baby's body for her to explore and watch which she chooses.

Toddlers

Coming to a decision is to make a deliberate choice, however, this is a time when young children also learn the word 'No!' They discover they have power and can challenge adults but also make things happen for themselves. They are spontaneous, curious, and eager to investigate and find out for themselves.

Practical activities

- Collect natural materials – stones, shells, wooden objects, cones – and display in baskets. Allow the children to handle them, sort them, and arrange them. Ask them to choose one of the objects that they like best. Extend this by encouraging them to talk about it by asking open questions such as 'What do you like about it?' 'Where do you think it has come from?' 'Does it remind you of anything?' Extend the activity by providing different-shaped shells of varying sizes and colours. Provide paints or modelling materials so that they can represent the shell in their own way.

- Make up outside play boxes to match the weather, for example 'A Windy Day Box', with windmill toys, streamers, sheets, clotheslines and pegs, flags. Let the children decide what they wish to play with. On return to the room talk about their choices and the feelings they experienced, such as the wind on their face, in their hair, the sounds they could hear. Make similar boxes for a sunny day, a rainy day and so on.

Outcomes for the child

- Experience of making choices supports later skills for making decisions.
- Positive choosing experiences supports being able to handle autonomy.
- Some choices have to be controlled/monitored by responsible adults.

Focus points

Some choices cannot be left to a baby or toddler because of health and safety. A good example of this is physical needs such as diet – babies and toddlers would probably choose to eat sweet things; however, a balanced diet is important for body growth. Drinking milk or water or having a nappy changed may not be desirable if the child is engrossed in play, but it may be physically advisable for comfort and ultimately for the child's well-being.

The team needs to be clear about the areas when health and safety dictate that choice may not be an option. For example, if a baby is sick and wet it is important she is cared for even though she may not express a wish to be changed.

Staff discussion

Audit toys and evaluate if there is sufficient choice, for example look at rattles and see if you can provide a wider range from which the children can then choose.

- How accessible are materials and toys to allow the children to make choices and decisions?
- Are there duplicate items available to avoid frustration or squabbles?
- Collect stories, songs and rhymes to extend children's play activities.

5. Being aware of others and their needs

As young children become more mobile and their boundaries widen, they make choices that can involve real risk. Adults need to ensure their safety, whilst not inhibiting risk taking

(Birth to Three Matters)

 Babies

Mobility is a breakthrough for babies and opens up choice for young children. As a baby learns to roll over it means she can be on her back or front. As soon as she begins to crawl and later walk it opens up a whole new world of choices – such as to go or stay, to hide or escape.

Practical activities

Carer–child ratios are in place to protect babies and toddlers as it is recognised their level of need and care is high. To begin the pathway to awareness that others have needs here are some suggestions:

- Provide a cosy area with cushions and soft flooring – a low level wicker basket which has duplicates of well loved books allows babies to grasp and pick up books.

- Place a 'treasure basket' on a soft bath mat with two babies, ensuring that the basket has duplicates of items appropriate for them. Act as a passive observer and note any gestures or non-verbal communication between them as they explore the treasures.

> **Caution:** Be aware that they have limited upper body control and so soft or rag books are safest when promoting shared book time.

Toddlers

Toddlers need to understand that some of their choices may create risks for others, and there may be consequences. Initially they will need guidance and support to understand the advantages and disadvantages of their actions. They need to develop empathy, 'walking a mile in someone else's shoes'.

Practical activities

- Use puppets to show situations where there is a possible safety risk. Ask the children what they can do to avoid the problem.

- Find stories that show situations where a character has been thoughtless or inconsiderate, for example 'Goldilocks'. Talk about how the bears felt when they came home. Ask what Goldilocks could have done differently.

- Encourage role-play situations where the children work collaboratively to help each other, such as getting out of a tunnel, or being lost in a wood. Play alongside and join in so that you can move the play forward.

- Help the children to learn about appropriate behaviour. Develop a few simple rules with them. Present a situation and ask the children to think about it. For example, one boy is happily riding a wheelie toy when another comes and pushes him off and grabs the trike. How does the first boy feel? What should the second boy have done?

- Write up the rules, preferably with a visual clue, and refer to them before free choice play.

Outcomes for the child

- Early awareness of others, interacting with their peers.
- Making a choice to communicate with others.
- Developing acceptable behaviour, caring for others.

Focus points

Boundaries are needed in terms of physical layout for safety but they should not be obtrusive and limiting. Once crawling babies tackle stairs and go up they realise innately that going down is different and make a different set of decisions on how they will go up and down. Babies are aware of other babies at certain times and for short periods. As they mature, they can be very aware of others but choose not to acknowledge them as their needs are the priority. If a child is upset, this is quickly picked up in a baby or toddler room and sometimes others copy the behaviour without understanding why they are doing it!

Toddlers need to understand what is acceptable behaviour. If they are unkind, selfish and do not care about others' needs they may not make any friends. They need to learn from a good role model so it is essential that the adults promote caring, thoughtful behaviour.

Staff discussion

- Discuss the steps a baby makes in becoming aware of others, for example when she realises she is separate from other people, when she learns to share and understand that others have feelings, when she is not over-anxious about new people and events, when she plays alongside others.

- Examine ways you could introduce the idea of 'Awareness of others' as a focus and for observations of social development.

- Are there ways you could promote good behaviour, thoughtfulness and caring for others?

6. Choosing the outdoors

Recognise that outdoor provision presents rich choices for babies and children and include this opportunity in your planning; e.g. streamers, bubbles and windmills in a windy day box

(Birth to Three Matters)

Babies

In order to be healthy, children need to experience the outdoor and natural world as this will offer a wider range of choices. Babies wrapped up warm in winter can have short bursts of time outside in their prams, and toddlers with the correct footwear and clothing can also benefit. At the other end of the spectrum, if it is hot outside playing can have benefits as long as there are protective hats and sun creams and cover such as a parasol. Access to water is key. Sensible amounts of time outside need careful consideration especially avoiding the midday sun or when the weather is particularly hot.

Practical activities

Opportunities that can be used to promote choices outside:

- Put out various textured mats and allow those babies who can crawl to investigate the different materials. The weather has to be fine and the surfaces dry and safe.

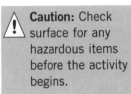

Caution: Check surface for any hazardous items before the activity begins.

- Let them choose a hat to wear – have a mirror (child safe) outside and let seated babies and crawlers try the different hats on and see how they look. A choice like this, which involves putting on and taking off items of clothing gives them experience of items they will put on later when they go outside for themselves.

- Push baby outside in a buggy and point to the trees in the wind, the birds in the air and then let babies hold simple small streamers and wave them, choosing from two or three kinds (perhaps one with crepe paper and another with shiny paper or just use simple ribbons).

- Have two books attached to the buggy and encourage babies to look and choose books outside.

Toddlers

The outdoors provides a rich multi-sensory environment, engaging all the senses and helping to develop and strengthen children's whole bodies. Toddlers can express themselves in vigorous or noisy activities that are not possible indoors or spend quiet, reflective moments watching a bird, feeling the wind on their face or tying ribbons to the fence. Benefits can be enhanced with the sensitive interaction of the adult carer. It is an ideal opportunity for a toddler to play at his own pace and self-direct his learning by deciding for himself what he wants to do.

Practical activities

- Provide low level equipment for balancing, climbing and sliding. Allow the children free choice or prepare a simple obstacle course.

- Give toddlers buckets for transporting sand, gravel and water. Support the close investigation of puddles.

- Provide baskets for the children to collect items that take their fancy such as leaves, flowers, feathers.

- Once inside arrange their favourite pieces on clear sticky back plastic then cover with another sheet or fix in between a clear plastic CD cover to make an instant picture.

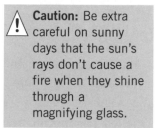 **Caution:** Ensure the objects are safe to handle and wash hands on return to indoors.

- Encourage the children to observe nature – supply magnifying glasses to investigate a flower, a seed pod, a worm or a small insect. Keep a range of simple information books or use the internet for the identification of flowers, birds and mini beasts.

Caution: Be extra careful on sunny days that the sun's rays don't cause a fire when they shine through a magnifying glass.

Outcomes for the child

- Seeing there are a range of options within a safe limit and to explore that range.
- Starting to build up personal likes and dislikes.
- Witnessing cause and effect – to learn some choices are good and some are bad.
- Developing a knowledge and understanding of nature.

Focus points

While the children are outside it is an ideal time for the adults to interact and engage in the children's learning. It is especially useful when dealing with a shy or reticent child. The adult can encourage him by joining in, playing alongside or becoming a partner. It is important that during this outside time the children learn to respect each other's wishes as well as all living things.

Staff discussion

- Observe how adventurous individual children are when playing outdoors. Do they like to climb, have a strong push on a swing?
- How do you end outdoor time? Do you encourage the toddlers to put the toys away?
- Do you end the outdoor time with a group activity to reconnect the children to the group? Look at the current ranges of outdoor resources and ask the question 'Is their enough variety to offer real choices and how do I present these to babies and toddlers?'

References

DfES (Department for Education and Skills) (2002) *Birth to Three Matters: A Framework to Support Children in their Earliest Years.* London: DfES.

DfES (Department for Education and Skills) (2003) *Every Child Matters.* London: DfES.

Ofsted (Office for Standards in Education)/DfES (Department for Education and Skills) (2003) *Full Day Care: Guidance to the National Standards.* London: DfES.

Resources

Hewett, A. (1999) *Mrs Mopple's Washing Line.* London: Red Fox.

Hohmann, M. and Weikart, D. (2002) *Educating Young Children: Active Learning Practices for Preschool and Child Care Programs.* Clinton, MI: High/Scope Educational Research Foundation.

Moyles, J. (1989) *Just Playing? The Role and Status of Play in Early Childhood.* Milton Keynes: Open University Press.

Paley, V. (1986) *Boys and Girls: Superheroes in the Doll Corner.* Chicago, IL: University of Chicago Press.

Pascal, C. and Bertram, A. (1997) *Effective Early Learning: 0 to 8 Years.* London: Hodder & Stoughton.

Conclusion

The aim for this book is to help early years practitioners and carers unpick the statements made on the *Birth to Three Matters* cards and to provide some practical ways to interpret and implement them.

The authors are experienced early years professionals who know and understand the realities of a busy setting. The suggested activities are tried and tested in real situations with real children and are reinforced by research, philosophy and legal requirements. The preceding chapters encourage the children to have a 'hands on' approach to learning but they are suggestions not a prescription. Every setting is different and every child is an individual with his own unique needs. The practitioner will be aware of the particular needs of her group and can take these suggestions and adapt them, developing them according to the diverse factors such as background, culture and children's stage of development.

It is a heavy responsibility to care for and educate vulnerable young children, keeping them safe, developing their growing bodies and minds while encouraging a basic foundation for a healthy lifestyle and a sense of well-being.

Appendix: The Birth to Three Framework for 'A Healthy Child'

A Healthy Child

Emotional Well-being

Emotional stability and resilience

Including
- Being special to someone
- Being able to express feelings
- Developing healthy dependence
- Developing healthy independence

Growing and Developing

Physical well-being

Including
- Being well nourished
- Being active rested and protected
- Gaining control of the body
- Acquiring physical skills

Keeping Safe

Being safe and protected

Including
- Discovering boundaries and limits
- Learning about rules
- Knowing when and how to ask for help
- Learning when to say no and anticipating when others will do so

Healthy Choices

Being able to make choices

Including
- Discovering and learning about his/her body
- Demonstrating individual preferences
- Making decisions
- Becoming aware of others and their needs

© DfES (2002) *Birth to Three Matters: A Framework to Support Children in their Earliest Years*